Decorating with
EVERGREENS

Decorating with EVERGREENS

❖

ROBERT WAITE

PHOTOGRAPHS BY ZAC WILLIAMS

GIBBS SMITH
TO ENRICH AND INSPIRE HUMANKIND

First Edition
15 14 13 12 11   5 4 3 2 1

Text © 2011 Robert Waite
Photographs © 2011 Zac Williams

Published by
Gibbs Smith
P.O. Box 667
Layton, Utah 84041

1.800.835.4993 orders
www.gibbs-smith.com

Designed by Sheryl Dickert
Printed and bound in Hong Kong

Gibbs Smith books are printed on paper produced
from sustainable PEFC-certified forest/controlled
wood source. Learn more at www.pefc.org.
Printed and bound in Hong Kong

Library of Congress Cataloging-in-
Publication Data available upon request

ISBN 13: 978-1-4236-2250-5

To LeAnn Arave and Anita Heaston for their invaluable help and their creative talents.
And to my beloved Rocky, my feline friend who brought such joy into my life.

CONTENTS

Introduction

❦

*N*othing says holidays like decorating with live evergreens.

This book will inspire you to celebrate the holidays in all their glory with the look and fragrance of evergreens. You will learn to combine different kinds of greenery including fir boughs, princess pine, juniper, and cedar to bring the holidays home. Whether it is a beautiful wreath for your front door, a magnificent centerpiece for your holiday table, or the Christmas tree by the fireplace, evergreens bring an ambiance and sense of celebration to the occasion. Their fragrance says holidays in a way nothing else can, and the live greenery in the midst of cold winter adds warmth and cheer and a hope for green growing things.

FACING: Designer Associates Floral is the fulfillment of a lifelong dream of the owner and designer, Robert Waite. Visitors to this shop can quickly sense his unique style of doing business.

LEFT: The front window boxes are changed several times a year to reflect the seasons and add a welcoming touch to this quaint little shop.

Author Robert Waite, owner of Designer Associates, shares his secrets of combining fresh flowers, fruit, and live greenery to create beautiful wreaths, swags, garlands, centerpieces, and more. These unexpected pieces incorporate juniper berries, fresh pomegranates, holly, ribbons, lotus pods, clementine oranges, pinecones, and wire spirals to create just the look and feel needed for each setting.

Waite's style is organic and inspired from the local and seasonal things at hand. He may include ivy from his backyard, sheaths of wheat from a nearby field, or crabapples from a neighbor's tree. Vases, pots, baskets, and unusual containers of all kinds help shape the arrangements. An old fishing creel or an antique milk pitcher lend their own unique style to a piece. His work and style encourages you to celebrate the slight imperfections and asymmetry in nature that allow the natural beauty to shine through. These arrangements show how different textures, weights, colors, and shapes can combine to create a feel from formal to casual, from cheery to reverent. All the arrangements evoke a sense of home and tradition, of holiday celebration, of joy and good will.

From antique ornaments to elaborate ribbons, from artichokes to fresh roses and berries, these beautiful, unusual arrangements will inspire and impress you. Bring the lushness of evergreens into your home for the holidays.

Inside Designer Associates you will find an eclectic mix of memorabilia and all the requirements of a working flower shop in a minimum of space. During the holidays the traditional Christmas box comes out. The box contains odds and ends that reflect the holiday themes waiting to be implemented into many arrangements.

ABOVE: A beautiful Jingle Bell poinsettia blossoms next to other fresh greenery and flower accents in this beautiful centerpiece.

FACING: Counters laden with a variety of floral arrangements awaiting delivery to the beautiful homes in the area, where they will add color and fragrances to the festive holiday décor.

Evergreens, fresh flowers, gourds, seed pods, pinecones, sticks, and berries are but a few of the items that might spark an idea for an arrangement.

WREATHS

Wreaths are one of the simplest of creations that can make a focal point of hospitality for a home. To hang a wreath on a door or house front is a warm and welcoming sign to greet both friends and family. Wreaths make a kind of bull's-eye for putting your home on the neighborhood map of friendliness. We hope that some of the ideas shown in this section will help inspire you as you begin your holiday decorating.

FACING: This grapevine wreath is in its simplest form, highlighted by a few evergreens and a whimsical polka-dot bow. Add some glass balls and you have an easy-to-make wreath.

RIGHT: Did someone say Mardi Gras? A grapevine wreath can be dressed up for any occasion. With a little bit of glitz and bling you are ready for the party to begin!

A wide variety of evergreens can be used to create unforgettable wreaths, which are so hearty they can survive harsh winters. Evergreen wreaths hanging outside in winter weather should last months and never need watering. Contrast that to an indoor Christmas tree that must be watered and will only survive weeks. In fact, evergreen wreaths hanging outside in cold weather will likely last longer than its owners may even want them too. They will probably outlive their welcome, as the seasons change.

Some people don't like the idea of holiday decorating before Halloween. But you can start looking around for items that you will be able to use in your holiday decorations ahead of the season. Keep your eyes open all year long, in fact. Have you ever heard of Christmas in July? There are many plants and flowers that you can pick in the summer and fall, and then hang them up to dry. Yarrow, statice, rose hips, pyracantha, sunflower pods, and black-eyed susan pods are just a few of numerous options. You need only to look right outside your door. A quick trip to the grocery store will provide nuts and fruits to give your creation color and interest. Some fruits can be sliced and dried, others give character just dried and shriveled.

The variety of greens you can use in arrangements is numerous as well. Fir, balsam, juniper, pine, and cedar are great standbys, as well as things like boxwood, magnolia, holly, eucalyptus, and salal, which can make great accents. We encourage you to use a combination of these materials in traditional and nontraditional ways.

Obviously artificial wreaths can be reused over and over and last for years. But you have to find somewhere to store them and, besides,

Concentric bands of color surround a large lotus pod in this eye-catching design, which adds a focal point to the lattice gate.

LEFT: A cute teddy bear Santa brings out the child in everyone. The addition of pinecones and wrapped presents round out this natural fir wreath.

FACING: Great wreaths can be made using what you have on hand. Starting with a basic evergreen wreath, add things from around your home. We found this wooden nutcracker, added the bow and balls, and make a striking piece.

you can't beat the wonderful fragrance of a freshly cut evergreen! If you have the tradition of a fresh-cut tree in your home, you can trim some of the lower branches and shape them into a wreath. Add a pretty bow and a few decorations on it, and you're all set.

Wreaths also offer a sharp contrast to some of today's high-tech holiday decorations that may require electric power or use LED energy-saving lights. Wreaths use no power and are among the simplest of holiday decorations available. Of course you could add lights if you desire; you will need an outlet nearby.

Unlike many Christmas decorations that may require hours to put in place, hanging a wreath can be done in just a few minutes, perhaps with just a single nail and piece of wire, ribbon, or twine. Some heavy-duty fishing line works also, and is virtually invisible. There are also wreath hangers, which hang

over the tops of doors and have a hook on the end for hanging the wreath. Within seconds you can hang your beautiful wreath on the hook. No nails required!

Wreaths can be hung just about anywhere—on a door or a window or the eaves of your home. They can be hung on the back of a chair, a stairwell, or on the wall of your home. You may also place them flat on a table as a centerpiece.

Wreaths make excellent preholiday gifts for friends, neighbors, and family. One man, who lives in the Seattle area, traditionally mails his mother a beautiful holiday wreath each year. She happily hangs it on her front door and leaves it hanging well into January.

Wreaths have an interesting history. The use of evergreen wreaths evolved from the use of an evergreen tree for the holidays. The Romans were probably first to use wreaths as both a sign of status and of victory. Laurel wreaths were worn by Greek Olympians as a sign of triumph. Anciently, women also wore small wreaths to show their pride, or as special decorations for weddings and other notable occasions.

FACING: This elegant antique fireplace mantel is the perfect setting for a wreath featuring an abundance of Clementine oranges, pinecones, and dried yellow statice.

LEFT: Magnolia leaves are a natural for this wreath that includes copper balls, aluminum wire twists, and pinecones. Magnolia leaves are a perfect choice for a wreath that you want to dry naturally to be used from year to year.

ABOVE: A natural grapevine wreath displays a cluster of pine and a variety of fruits, seeds, and pods.

FACING: Any wall, interior or exterior, can be enhanced by the addition of holiday color, as shown with this wreath with its tiny presents and holly against the rough shingle wall.

The word *wreath* originated from the Old English "writha," and evolved in Middle English to "wrethe," meaning a twisted ring of flowers made into a garland.

It was during the Middle Ages when evergreens really caught on for holiday decorating. Candles were often added by Christians on their early evergreen wreaths, one a day or one a week until December 25, when the last candle was added to symbolize the birth of Jesus Christ.

In more modern times, wreaths at Christmastime have come to be a symbol of Jesus Christ's eternal love. An evergreen, a durable plant that has much longevity, also seems perfect in Christianity as a symbol that represents immortality, which followers of Christ strive for. The circular shape of wreaths can also be connected as a symbol of eternity, without beginning or end. Fruits or colors added to the wreath can denote the rich variety of God's creations. Even the prickly holly has its symbolism and is supposed to remind Christians of the crown of thorns.

FACING: Starting with a water foam base, this wreath is greened with salal, juniper, ming fern, and holly. Then white miniature carnations and limonium are added to make it really pop.

RIGHT: Princess pine, rose hips, curly cane, and lotus pods provide a natural habitat for the bright red cardinals.

Evergreens are also surprising in that they remain alive in winter and can even still bear fruit in bitter cold. So, in one sense, they are truly the sign of life in the winter season. In times past, this hope of renewed life was particularly important when there was no electric or gas heat and winters could truly be harsh times. Even today in the dead of winter, people need hope and a reminder of spring.

Whether or not you have religious inclinations, wreaths convey a hometown charm for the holidays. They are a timeless symbol of love and friendship. Indeed, technologies will expand by leaps and bounds over the ages ahead, but wreaths will remain, their warm, inviting legacy a reminder of holidays and warmth, family, and friends.

LEFT: A wreath will brighten up any place you choose to call home.

FACING: The abundance of the season is exemplified by this bay leaf wreath with clusters of wheat, red and yellow apples, and cranberry-colored dried yarrow.

BELOW: Boxwood and Christmas
ribbon make a classic wreath.

FACING: A traditional plaid ribbon and
pepper berries make this variegated natural
evergreen wreath festive and fun.

FACING: A treasured memento invites all who enter to join in the fun. This antique sled is surrounded by a very large fir and juniper wreath. A large gold and burgundy bow completes the welcome.

RIGHT: Red berry garlands drape this wreath of natural firs and pinecones. The glass snowflakes add a bit of sparkle.

GARLANDS AND MANTELS

D uring the time of the early American settlers, life was dominated by the fireplace, which was used for cooking, heating, and illumination. The fireplace became the focal point of family living, especially during the winter months. The mantel above the fireplace served as a shelf for essential items used in everyday life, such as candles and other practical implements.

Eventually the fireplace mantel became the centerpiece of the coziest room in the home—especially during the holiday season. It is the perfect place to gather round, as you invite your family and friends to enjoy a beautiful, warm setting to celebrate the holidays.

This lovingly restored fireplace is the perfect setting for a natural evergreen mantelpiece. Pinecones, acorns, cranberries, dried yarrow, and a red berry garland contribute to a pleasing, natural look.

ABOVE: A collection of cherished nutcrackers is prominently displayed on this mantelpiece and completed with a variety of nuts, red satin balls, gold seeded eucalyptus, and pinecones. This arrangement is sure to be a conversation starter.

FACING: This glistening mantelpiece, covered with an assortment of brightly colored Christmas ornaments, is reflected in the mirror at the senior citizen center, adding to the holiday atmosphere.

When decorating a mantel, you may want to look around your room. Decide if you want to accent what you already have or start with new things. Mantels are a great place to display treasured items, but they can easily become cluttered and messy if not given the proper attention. If you have a collection of nutcrackers, you could display them, and add some evergreens, balls, or berries for a meaningful and simple mantel display.

There are no real rules to decorating a mantel. If it is pleasing to the eye and brings warmth and comfort to your room, then you have succeeded. Some people think more along the lines of symmetry, which can denote more formality, while other people are drawn to asymmetry, which is more relaxed. If the room is formal, a symmetrical display may work best. A casual room may benefit from an asymmetrical grouping. Often a rule of thumb in decorating and styling is that grouping items in odd numbers is always more pleasing to the eye. So, a grouping of three decorative vases will look better than two, as will five candlesticks look better than four.

The entire area of the fireplace can have accents and decorations. The mantel, above the mantel, and the hearth can all be decorated to coordinate. The items used in a fireplace mantel display should complement the style of the room as a whole. That's not to say that there isn't room for contrast. An unexpected object can always add interest—just don't overdo it.

Some traditions include the hanging of Christmas stockings from the mantel. One legend tells of a nobleman who lost his wife and his fortune, leaving his three daughters poor and without a dowry. One evening, after the sisters had hung their stockings to dry by the fireplace, St. Nicholas happened by their cottage on his horse. Seeing the empty socks, he tossed three bags of gold down the chimney and into the stockings, to the joy of the family. Legends from other countries tell about leaving wooden shoes or stockings by the hearth to find them full of fruits, nuts, and candy the next morning.

When decorating your mantel or fireplace hearth, keep in mind that if you are using the fireplace to heat your home often and it tends to get really warm, so keep your decorations at a distance so you won't melt them or start them on fire.

FACING: Poinsettias adorn both the mantelpiece and hearth of this rustic stone fireplace.

RIGHT: Three centerpieces featuring evergreens, holly, red miniature carnations, and scotch broom surround white metal luminaries in which tea lights illuminate the holiday sentiments *joy, peace,* and *noel.*

LEFT: Burgundy and gold are the strikingly dominant colors in this elegant arrangement featuring artificial grape clusters, pinecones, gold aluminum wire twists, and slender burgundy tapers. The rich satin ribbon is both tied in bows and draped throughout the arrangement.

FACING: Glittery red and gold stars, wrapped gifts, and mesh ribbon bows stand atop cedar evergreens gracefully draped with natural seed pods and pinecones on this magnificent historic fireplace.

FACING: This mantel arrangement is as timeless in feel as the old clock that welcomes visitors to the Sommer home. Foxtails, apples, and pepper berries are joined by pinecones and gold bead garlands to good effect.

ABOVE: The clean and simple design of this fireplace is beautifully enhanced by the warm colors and natural textures of this arrangement.

A combination of princess pine, juniper, and fir boughs needed only the addition of lotus pods, sticks, red berry clusters, and cardinals to add inspiration to the beauty of this room.

Garlands are perfectly suited to mantelpieces. The Christmas garland history tells us that the early settlers to America brought the custom of Christmas garlands, also called Christmas ropes, when they immigrated. Making and selling Christmas garlands added to the family's income. The garlands were used to decorate Christmas trees and for other adornment purposes, decorating a room or the outside of a house during Christmas season.

A garland can be made of anything that drapes. It can be made out of the same types of evergreens wreaths are made of, such as cedar, spruce, pine, balsam, fir, and so on. Garlands can be made as full or as thin as you wish. In addition to evergreens, garlands can be made out of dried fruits, popcorn, berries, and nuts. These types of garlands can be intertwined with evergreen garlands to add color and dimension.

FACING: This richly carved banister in the entryway of the Hill home is enriched with a lavish display of fresh cedar garlands, pinecones, hypericum berries, gold seeded eucalyptus, and a luxurious satin bow.

LEFT: The end post creates a pedestal for a dramatic arrangement of all of the elements used to decorate the banister, and adds cardinal red roses, safari sunset, and glitter-covered balls.

LEFT: The cedar garland winds its way upward to
the second landing of this stately stairway.

ABOVE: A pleasing combination of the beauties
of nature and the warm luster of wood.

FACING: The Reese family celebrates
Christmas while in the process of restoring
their beautiful historic home.

ABOVE: This cedar garland is embellished
with clusters of pinecones, blue and silver
balls, and patterned satin ribbon, as it
cascades to the floor in the hall.

The second floor of the Simpson
home gives a glimpse of the
holiday splendor waiting below.

LEFT: A large bow with ribbon streamers marks the beginning of the stairway.

FACING: This exquisitely restored stairway is draped with ropes of fresh cedar and holiday ribbon. Groupings of pinecones and bright red apples bring unity to the entire entryway.

The white picket fence that surrounds the Robert Waite home features a scalloped draping of cedar garland. Each post is topped with bows of yellow and his favorite apple green.

A simple ribbon tied up in certain spots, to make a drape, can then be adorned with clusters of evergreens, pinecones, berries, and bows. Make garlands simple or elegant, depending on the area you are decorating.

You can place a garland above the mantel, nestled on the mantel, or draped below it if you are not having a fire in the fireplace. Garlands can be used to accentuate a window or doorway, or placed above an archway in a home. A stairway is a beautiful place to hang a garland. To enhance the craftsmanship of an elegant wooden banister, an evergreen garland serves as a dramatic accent. Tie on some ribbons and bows, add fruit, flowers, or pinecones, and you have a masterpiece.

Garlands can also be placed outdoors. A fence draped with a beautiful evergreen garland will welcome your friends and family to your home. Green garlands make an especially attractive picture when contrasted with a white snow-covered ground. They can be placed along the railing leading the way to your door and then continue around the doorway.

Christmas garlands are not only for home decoration. Garlands are beautiful in public spaces such as churches, businesses, shops, and restaurants. They add a sense of community and shared celebration of the holidays.

The Christmas garland is one of the most versatile holiday decorations. Nothing can compensate for the inviting smell of fresh evergreens in the home during the cold, bleak winter months. So make it as simple or elegant as you like. And bring some of the old traditions of warmth to your home while building new traditions as well.

The simple beauty of fresh evergreen garland with pinecones, red bows, and berries are all that is needed to bring holiday reverence to this magnificent tabernacle.

LEFT: The red sandstone brick exterior wall on this home is the perfect backdrop for an arch of fir and juniper, red glazed apples, pinecones, berry sprays, and designer ribbon.

FACING: A fir arch sparkles with swags of gold mesh glitter stars in this Victorian parlor.

HOLIDAY CENTERPIECES

*P*erhaps the most exciting of any holiday decoration is the centerpiece. Throughout history, the large feasts in all the European countries featured the centerpiece and it has carried on to the present day. In eighteenth century America, the rich and well-to-do competed to have the most beautifully decorated table. The word *centerpiece* infers that it is the center of attention, and much creativity and imagination is put into making beautiful centerpieces.

FACING: A beautifully crafted pine and holly centerpiece, with carnations and feverfew, brings a holiday feel to any room.

LEFT: Green apples, variegated holly, and princess pine in a fireside basket grace a kitchen counter.

Anciently, the Romans and Greeks used massive amounts of greenery, fruit, and even the subject of the feast—for example, the roasted pig—as centerpieces. Today, the centerpiece is largely used to make the table cheerful, attractive, and inviting. An appropriate centerpiece brings all the hope of Christmas alive! It fills the room with the sweet aroma of fresh evergreen and bright colors to show off a beautiful table.

Something simple is often the most effective. Take the time to choose an unusual or interesting container. We pride ourselves on finding very unique items. Use an old pot, bowl, basket, box, or other unusual container and fill it with greens and berries. How about an old water can? Or a basket overflowing with evergreens and fruit? Instead of a favorite vase or urn, employ a pretty household item, such as a sugar bowl or teapot, and then fill it with flowers that show it off. You can even simply lay some greenery down the middle of the table add fresh fruit and nuts or circle greenery around a large bowl of soup or punch that you are serving.

For most of us, our décor may be limited by our budget. Use this constraint as a source for creativity, rather than something that holds you back. Why not think green? Gather greens from around your yard.

Citrus oranges are simply presented here with evergreens
topped by a lotus pod and a Ting Ting accent.

ABOVE: A Christmas basket medley of apples, citrus, and other fruits, cones, and pine makes a wonderful holiday delight.

FACING: A woody, earthy feel is evoked with safari sunset and rose hips set on this wood butcher block in a rustic kitchen.

Decorating with garland or boughs of greenery not only looks festive but can be done at a fraction of the cost of some readymade decorations. Take a look outside. What do you see? Anything from pine and cedar to holly and ivy can be used for holiday decorating. When properly cared for, many types of evergreens can last several weeks indoors.

Cutting boughs from your own trees or shrubs is not just economical; it can also be good for them. Some cedar trees, for example, are by

FACING: A beautiful swan arrangement in Kay Blood's dressing room denotes joy and the romance of a Dickensian Christmas.

LEFT: A silver bowl filled with evergreens, a variety of fresh flowers, eucalyptus, and fuchsia-colored aluminum wire twists is an elegant holiday centerpiece.

The bathroom is also entitled to a little joy and cheer. Here the combination of pine and eucalyptus brings in a nice fragrance.

nature a little thin, and pruning the tips helps them grow back fuller. Evergreens that have needles should not be heavily pruned. If you cut a pine tree branch to the trunk it will not grow back, but you can safely trim the smaller branches down to the main branch, shaping the tree as you go.

The cut evergreens will either dry beautifully or stay lush and supple for about three weeks, long enough to get through the holidays. And they last even longer if they are used outdoors or set in water. The natural charm of evergreens can offer wonderful, fresh fragrances too.

In addition to greenery, you can dress up your evergreen décor with other landscape items. For instance, you are sure to come across a variety of berries, nuts, and acorns. You can also use moss, pinecones, dried flowers, and seedpods. Gather pinecones and arrange them in a basket for a simple centerpiece. Flowers may not last as long as evergreens, but they can bring in some beautiful colors and variety to your arrangement. Use the season's traditional blooms, or other favorite flower.

Do centerpieces only belong in the center of your table? No! A centerpiece can be an arrangement anywhere you want to draw attention to. They can brighten up a foyer or an entry hall. A beautiful piece of antique furniture with a lovely arrangement on it makes a wonderful focal point to a room. A large basket with greens, pinecones, and holly berries sitting on the fireplace hearth is very inviting. Nostalgic memories of yesteryear can be created by decorating with holiday centerpieces and evokes the feeling of "I'll be home for Christmas."

This unique holiday basket cradles a poinsettia with ivy, pine, carnations, seeded eucalyptus, and red berries.

FACING: An elegant glass vase with fresh pine, white stargazer
lilies, variegated carnations, and red seeded eucalyptus
give the perfect focus to this antique sofa table.

ABOVE: Lotus pods with princess pine and ivy, and
fresh daisy mums, on the parlor table.

LEFT: An old roll-top desk is made beautiful with a simple goblet filled with pine, pepper berries, lisianthus, and glass balls.

FACING: A Jingle Bell poinsettia is simplicity itself. An evergreen wreath surrounds its base.

FACING: A milk stool
in front of the fireplace,
with a Christmas basket,
makes a cozy area.

RIGHT: Lime green spider
mums, hot pink roses,
and princess pine make
up this arrangement.

ABOVE: Princess pine, cedar, sprengeri, carnations, cones, copper balls, and lotus pods bring warmth to this hearth.

FACING: Santa's sleigh filled with cedar and princess pine, decorative ornaments, white alstromeria, and holly.

FACING: Yellow enchantment lilies, sprengeri, magnolia leaves, and red roses are among the flowers in this presentation.

ABOVE: Citrus, tulips, yellow pixie carnations, and spider mums grace this distinctive lime green container. Christmas arrangements need not always be the traditional red and green.

DOORS AND WINDOW TREATMENTS

———◆◆◆———

ecorating doors has early beginnings in the history of mankind. The Druids used sprigs of evergreen holly in the house. To them, it meant eternal life. The Norsemen felt that the evergreen symbolized the revival of the sun god Balder. Those who believed in superstition would put branches of evergreens over their doors to keep out witches, ghosts, and evil spirits. Decorating doors has been done for centuries. The Romans are believed to be the first culture to decorate the front door with wreaths during times of celebration and used the wreath to symbolize royalty and achievement. For the northern cultures, evergreens signified hope and a new light toward the coming spring.

FACING: Twin door swags reflect the colors of this vintage home.

LEFT: An old wicker lantern was the inspiration for this door hanger composed of evergreens, pinecones, birch sticks, and berries with a plaid holiday ribbon.

A focal point of decorating for any holiday should be the door; after all, the door is where everyone passes through into your home. At Thanksgiving, it is a great place to put a wreath or arrangement with fruits and gourds or other expressions of bounty. When Christmas comes it is time to indulge in the spirit of the holiday and welcome everyone wholeheartedly into your home. One of the most fun-filled activities related to Christmas can be decorating your house, inside and out.

The entrance to your home sets the stage for family, friends, and neighbors to join in the festivities you have planned for the season. The front door is the very first impression people get. Your entrance announces to the outside world the spirit of celebration inside.

RIGHT: A welcoming invitation to enter the Reeses's front door may be very similar to those extended when the home was owned by John R. Barnes.

FACING: Among the most interesting features of this large door treatment are the wide variety of evergreens and the clusters of rose-colored grapes.

Decor does not have to be complicated—using your imagination and creativity is all you need to make a door treatment. You can decorate the whole doorway or entryway, wrap a garland around the doorframe, hang a wreath or swag on the door itself, or set a basket of evergreens and pinecones next to the door. Drape another garland along the railing leading to your entry. Window boxes can also be transformed into decorative highlights.

LEFT: A wrought iron pot holder is a fun find from an estate sale. It is incorporated into a piece that now beckons holiday guests to this home.

ABOVE: The serenity of this front porch is reflected in the simple bundle of natural materials tied with a bow to make a swag arrangement.

FACING: No matter the season or weather, a luscious door swag is always a welcome sign.

ABOVE: The local grocery store can provide inspiration for arrangements in the form of artichokes, pomegranates, and juicy apples.

FACING: Simplicity is the key to this diminutive seasonal swag comprised of straight and curly Tings, juniper and princess pine, pyracantha berries, and woven green ribbon with a single miniature pumpkin.

BELOW: The delicate "s" curve of this pine and holly swag adds a gentle note to the season.

FACING: The vibrant red doorway of artist LeConte Stewart's studio provides a rich backdrop for this heavenly piece.

ABOVE: The softly curved lines of this door hanging are present in both the drape of the princess pine and the polished brass moons.

Swags are a just a grouping of pine boughs tied together at the top, with some ribbon or just about anything you would like to add to it. Hang a swag on the door, off to the side of the door, along the railing, or on a post of the porch.

Garlands, wreaths, ribbons, and bows all make for a bright, cheerful welcome and add warmth and peaceful living on a cold December day. Door and window treatments say "Welcome friends and all who enter!"

From the garden gate, down the walkway, up some stairs, and until you reach the finale—the front door—holiday decorations can be used as a focal point that will let everyone know that your home delights in the season and even strangers are wished the best of holiday cheer.

Start with a bunch of angel vine twigs, then add swaths
of lime green mesh, lotus pods, acorns, privet berries, and
purple heather to create this light and airy swag.

A very traditional Christmas swag, this piece is a simple grouping of pine boughs, pinecones, and berries finished with a holiday bow.

The unique find of a fishing creel can
be made into a work of art with fruits,
pods, berries, and pine boughs.

LEFT: The most arresting feature of this oval-shaped panel is the dried red clover paired with a red-and-white plaid bow.

FACING: Pepper berries added to any Christmas décor will dry naturally and maintain their wonderful color.

LEFT: Pine flocked to look like it's covered in snow makes a lovely presentation for this window box. Use your imagination to add almost anything as you create your own style of Christmas decorations.

ABOVE: Two wreaths in one: a traditional pine wreath encircles multicolored Christmas ornaments.

FACING: This one-of-a-kind door almost becomes part of the arrangement. The red glass balls and wrapped presents make this basket filled with evergreens and holly really stand out.

RIGHT: The charming entrance to the LeConte Stewart home, a Utah Historic Site, truly reflects the heart of an artist.

BELOW: Christmas ornaments in a multitude of colors, complemented by a gold bow and Christmas greens, add luster to this out-of-the-ordinary front door.

FACING: The granary of the Alan and Kay Blood home becomes a fitting showcase for this stunning plaque of unusually shaped gourds, pyracantha berries, and autumn leaves. The evergreen mix enlivens the arrangement, and the basswood sticks add dimension and flare.

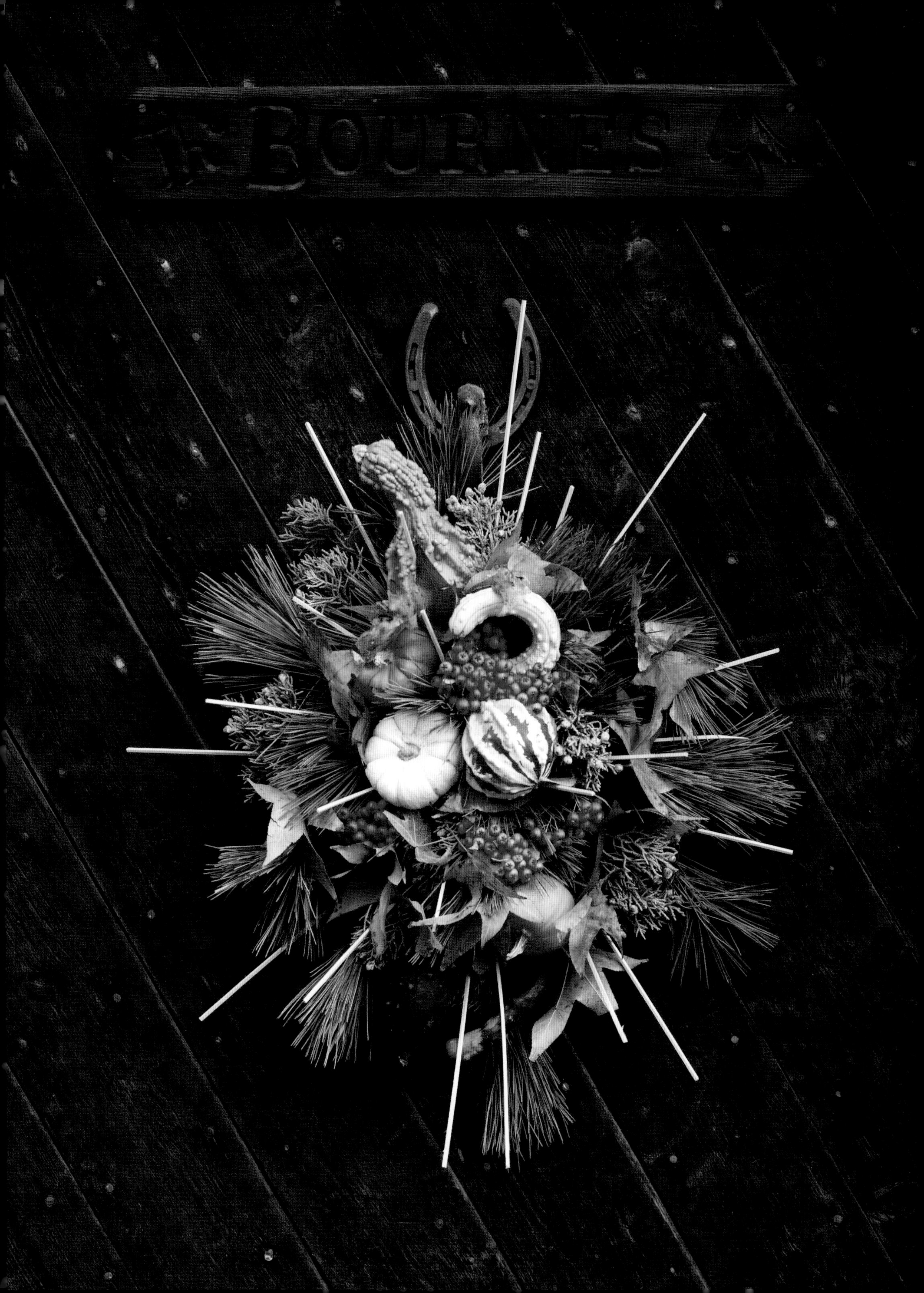
BOURNE'S

CHRISTMAS TREES

❧

The fir tree has a long association with Christianity. It began in Germany almost a thousand years ago when St. Boniface, who converted the German people to Christianity, was said to have come across a group of pagans worshipping an oak tree. In anger, St. Boniface cut down the oak tree and to his amazement a young fir tree sprang up from the roots of the tree. St. Boniface took this as a sign of the Christian faith. But it was not until the sixteenth century that fir trees were brought indoors at Christmastime.

FACING: Berries and twigs along with the miniature lights provide a warm and homey feel. Grapevine garlands spiral around the tree and small nests are provided for the birds, all of which makes a very natural scene.

LEFT: Red berries, a red cardinal, and birch twigs in a close-up view of a Spruce treetop.

Late in the Middle Ages, Germans and Scandinavians placed evergreen trees inside their homes or just outside their doors to show their hope in the forthcoming spring. Our modern Christmas tree evolved from these early traditions.

Legend has it that Martin Luther began the tradition of decorating trees to celebrate Christmas. One crisp Christmas Eve, about the year 1500, he was walking through snow-covered woods and was struck by the beauty of a group of small evergreens. Their branches, dusted with snow, shimmered in the moonlight. When he got home, he set up a little fir tree indoors so he could share this story with his children. He decorated it with candles, which he lighted in honor of Christ's birth.

By the 1830s, the evergreen tree had invaded British holiday traditions. It is told that the Christmas tree was brought to England by Queen Victoria's husband, Prince Albert, from his native Germany. There is a famous etching, from 1848, featuring the royal family of Victoria, Albert, and their children gathered around a Christmas tree in Windsor Castle. This popularized the tree throughout Victorian England.

About the same time, the Christmas tree also became a popular fixture in America. Formally decorated Christmas trees in America do not go back as far as you might imagine. Charles Follen, a German immigrant and professor at Harvard, was the first American on record to decorate a Christmas tree, an evergreen, in America, in the year 1832. His decoration caught on and other Americans began to do the same each year.

This old-fashioned tree, with multicolored cracked glass balls rescued from a yard sale and cascading ribbon, evokes a pleasant feeling of Christmases past. The vintage Free Spirit Bicycle makes the perfect addition to the scene.

LEFT: An evergreen tree with snowflakes, stars, and glittery balls spells out peace on earth.

FACING: Snowflake décor helps with a "hibernal ambiance." Limiting colors to silver and gold brings a wintery feeling to the celebratory tree.

But the custom spread slowly. The Puritans banned Christmas in New England. Even as late as 1851, a Cleveland minister nearly lost his job because he allowed a tree in his church. Schools in Boston stayed open on Christmas Day through 1870, and sometimes expelled students who stayed home for the holiday.

Christmas tree farms sprang up during the Depression. During this time, nurserymen couldn't sell their evergreens for landscaping, so they cut them for Christmas trees. Cultivated trees were preferred because they have more symmetrical shapes then wild ones.

The Christmas tree is a symbol of the living Christmas spirit and brings into our lives a pleasant aroma of the forest. It is truly the "tree of life and hope" in a dreary world of frustrations and helplessness.

While the Christmas tree is the center of our holiday decorations, adorned with all kinds of ornaments, lights, and even imitation snow, it was first used in the medieval German paradis plays that

ABOVE: The burgundy ribbons enhance the tree with warmth and the aluminum spirals add sparkle.

FACING: Placing the lighting beneath the metallic ribbon causes a subdued glow and makes this vary sparse tree into a holiday splendor.

portrayed the creation of humankind. This tree of life was a fir tree decorated with apples. Later paper flowers and other ornaments were added.

People often have the Christmas trees as the focal point of their room, with presents underneath. However, there are many ways to incorporate a Christmas tree into your space. Very small trees can be placed on kitchen countertops or cabinets to dress up the kitchen. They can be decorated with berries or small fruits. The dining room is a great place to add an additional tree. A slender Christmas tree in the corner, or a small tabletop tree placed on a hutch, sideboard, or small table will add decorative excitement to your celebration. The entire room will sparkle with joy and celebration. The entrance hall is another perfect place for a Christmas tree. It will shout "Merry Christmas" to everyone who enters the front door.

If you're decorating on a budget, you can use ribbons and bows instead of expensive ornaments. This will add elegance and charm without breaking the bank. Plan ahead and buy ribbon when it's on sale to make your own bows. Check out local thrift shops, yard sales, or antique stores to find unusual and inexpensive ornaments. A little Christmas tree in every room will wish everyone a very Merry Christmas!

FACING: A front porch display evokes our childlike delight in all things Christmas.

LEFT: Wrapped gifts and a Santa teddy bear create a fun and playful mood for the holidays.

As the sun goes down and
the lights come on, the tree
takes on a magic all its own.

This vintage caravan trailer is spectacularly enhanced by a fresh Christmas wreath and a beautiful pinion pine.

Acknowledgments

I'd like to thank the following folks who allowed us into their beautiful homes for this project. Without them this book would not have been possible.

Lynn Arave

Richard and Loraine Bourne

Margaret Brough

Dennis and Genene Hill

Lance and Nancy Reese

Norris and Dale Robins

Scott and Samantha Simpson

Gibbs and Catherine Smith

Paul and Amanda Sommer

Lorin and Kaye Wild

Kaysville First Ward

I also want to thank Gibbs Smith who encouraged me to do this project. Also Kirk Ziegler who helped me put the words together and my darling sister Rula Hunter.

Reference Guide

———◆◆◆◆◆———

You can purchase most of your flowers, evergreens, and other basic items needed for your arrangements from your local florist or garden center. You will also find additional items, such as containers, at hardware, variety, and thrift stores. Yard sales are a great resource for unusual, one-of-a-kind pieces for very little cost. Supermarkets, ceramic shops, and department stores are also great resources. For unusual items, or just for fun, go on an adventure in neighboring fields, woods, or countryside. You never know what weeds or windfalls you will find that will make the perfect addition to your arrangement.

The following supplier will provide a catalog upon request:

Denver Wholesale Florist Company
4800 Dahlia St.
P.O. Box 1138
Denver, Colorado 80201